Ramblings of a Stranger

Rachael Hiscock

BookLeaf Publishing
India | USA | UK

Presentation by *BookLeaf Publishing*

Web: www.bookleafpub.com

E-mail: info@bookleafpub.com

ISBN: 9789358316568

First edition 2023

In loving memory of;

Elijah Freddie Hiscock

Born Sleeping

14.06.2023

ACKNOWLEDGEMENT

My husband for putting up with me
My son for being my biggest cheerleader.
My mum for pushing me into this and always believing in me.

PREFACE

I've wrote a collection of poetry based on life events. The emotions are raw and its based on real life. From marriage to loss and the people I've met along the way.
I hope it resonates with some of you.

For every sale of this book I will donate a percentage to a charity called 4louis who helped us through the hardest time.
So when you buy this book you're helping bereaved families after baby loss.

Who am I?

I'm a woman who's 33
And still not sure what to be
I'm a mother, I'm a wife.
I've tried a few different paths in life.

I enjoy reading, country music,and French fries.
I'm a little under tall and have brown eyes.
I've written poetry about life and significant events.
A therapy that has brought me to feeling content.

You and I are strangers now, but I'm about to let you in.
I'll take you on the journey if your ready. Let's begin.

I was a single mum at twenty-one.
People said my life was over before it had begun.
My son was diagnosed with autism at the age of five.
The years leading up to that I'd just about survived.
When my son was seven, I met the man I would marry.

All I cared about right then was he made us both so happy.
I worked for a while in the NHS
Helped people in a time of need and distress
Then I headed up a forum to champion policies for our kids.
Speaking out for parent carers, running events and writing bids.
Then I started working back in health and linked up with Autistic adult care
That brings us up to now and I am still there.

I had another baby, born in June 2023.
I lost myself a little then because it wasn't to be
My son was born to the angels 5 days after our wedding day
Shock and sadness descended. We really lost our way.
I wrote through all these journeys and I share them in this book.
So if you want to know more, read on, take a look.
I am just a woman who is now 33
Writing about experiences that made me, me!

A mother daughter thing...

In a world where love takes flight,
A bond of strength, forever bright,
A mother and daughter, hand in hand,
Guiding each other across life's vast land.

With every heartbeat, a rhythm shared,
A connection deep, beyond compare,
A mother's love, fierce and true,
Nurturing her daughter, helping her through.

She's a beacon of wisdom, a guiding light,
Teaching lessons, both day and night,
Through laughter, tears, and joyous embrace,
A mother's love leaves no empty space.

Together they weather every storm,
Through highs and lows, their hearts warm,
From gentle whispers to words unspoken,
Their love, an eternal bond unbroken.

Across the years their friendship grew
Not sure now who is who.
Always together never alone
Only ever at the end of a phone.

Chaos and laughter ensues wherever they go
From shopping, to hospitals they always know
As long as they have each other they will be
alright
Mum is there to help with every fight

For in this dance of life they partake,
A mother's love, a daughter does make
The tapestry they weave, a masterpiece,
A bond of love that will never cease.
With love for
my wonderful mam

The Black Dog

I wish you knew how hard is is to make it through each day
when every situation throws something new my way.
I dont like uncertainty I like things planned ahead
so being in new situations is a time i've come to dread.

If you saw me before this then how different things would be
before it all changed within me this is what you'd see

Someone who will support you from beginning to the end
someone who is honest and doesn't do pretend.
Someone who is loyal and has your best interests at heart
someone who will remember things whether near or apart.

You would find I could be funny and really have some fun
I was pretty easy going and never felt quite done

I'd do anything for my real friends but not be taken for a fool
I had a brain I wasn't afraid of and did pretty well at school

That is in the past, it's not what you see right now
I dont like where i'm at and I really dont know how!
How I came to be here and feel the way I do
and why I now believe that all I was just isn't true!

I never know if what I do is right or if it's not
I'm sometimes innaproriate and can be quite a lot
I never feel quite good enough and the pressure it is real
I just want to be my old self and tell you how I feel.
I'm scared to let anyone get too close to me
because i am unsure of what would happen you see.

It's not that I dont want you, in fact the opposite is true
but I feel I dont deserve you, so I tell you that we're through.
What you see on social media, it is not who I am

when you see me in the pictures and you think
my life is glam.

I never feel like I deserve something that could
be this right
and I certainly shouldn't have it without a
substantial fight.
The thing is though I'm tired, tired in my mind
running round in circles searching for answers
i'll never find.
You will never stay with me when you see what
you could have had
and I totally don't blame you so please do not
feel bad.
The suspicions and accusations are much to
much to bare
and I know that what i'm doing is really not too
fair.

How I am is not a choice believe me when I say
i'd do pretty much anything to be a different
way.
I'm a victim of an illness that no one else can see
but it poisons me and suffocates the person I
want to be

I do all I can to take control, to be ready for the
fight

but when your used to losing you dont give it all
you might.

Everybody tells me that i'm crazy and I know
that its true
but this goes way beyond the usual feeling blue.
I don't know why I feel this way and I wish that
it would stop.
That I could see my life as others do instead of it
feeling like a flop.

I'm not the girl whose confident and strutting
round the floor
I'm not the girl thats dancing taking selfies, shots
and more
i'm not the girl you see laughing and messing
around
i'm not the girl who's gossiping about some info
I have found.

I am all the things i've told you, but you do not
believe!
Careful what you're doing looks can so easily
decieve!

I'm not really sure of what I am at this point in
time
I need to be reminded of the things that made
you mine.

It's always easier to see all the things i'm not
but all the things that made me good I seem to
have forgot.

Depression: it is not a choice and it does not
discriminate,
it sneaked up on me slowly,
I didnt feel its weight!
Until it took every bit of joy, and turned it into
hate.

Infertility = Inadequacy

Secondary infertility is really hard
People think you can have more but won't
They tell you, you should and groan when you don't
They don't see the commitment day after day
Temping and tracking in every way.
Special diets, more exercise, mindfulness and holistic
Then someone says do you not want another because your first is Autistic
The periods come month after month they trick you when they take longer it's a punch to the gut
You smile and reply politely to people who pry
They will never know the strength it took for you not to cry.

You cling to the child your so blessed to have you don't want them to grow.
It's a selfish thought as you well know.
You may never see this stage again and it brings both joy and pain.
The period cramps seem crueller somehow
When you've wished them not to come so many times now
You try to be strong don't go around moping

But somedays it's so hard you're barely coping.
So you cry silent tears alone in your room
While hating yourself and cursing your womb
You ache for yourself and your partner too who
wants this baby just as much as you.
The doctors say there's no reason why, and all
you can do is continue to try

It feels like a punishment but you don't know the
crime
And your serving it out over an indeterminate
time.
You try to distract get the thoughts out your head
sometimes it's just too much when you fall into
bed
Babies and pregnancy are everywhere you look
your getting flashbacks of the negative test you
took
We all live in hope even if we're hit with despair
Why is this happening it just isn't fair!

Miscarriage

I looked at the stick i held in my hand
With two lines on sonbold and grand
Something we'd longed for many times now
Was finally coming true somehow
Excitement took over we were looking forward
with glee
We weren't to know it was not going to be
I took the tablets ate all the right things. And
vowed to embrace pregnancy and all that it
brings
Every trial and tribulation would be worth it i
knew
To be blessed with our miracle-you
I woke up one morning feeling not right
Found blood in my knickers red and bright
Panicked I didn't know what to do
Please god please don't let this be true
Make it stop I'm begging you.
A scan revealed what we knew all along
It was too late you were already gone
Gone before many even knew you were here
But to us little one you were precious and dear.
We had photos we wanted to take
Plans and memories we wanted to make
Decorate the nursery with your name on the wall

But the bigger the dreams the further the fall
Now I'm sitting alone with no tears left to shed
The memory of it all dancing round in my head
At least you can get pregnant they say
But it took 2 long years and we felt everyday
Try again right away it's the best idea
It could happen quickly you were so near
I wasn't near i was already there
Wiping your face and brushing your hair
Now your gone there's nothing left to do
Except try to move on with the memory of you
Our almost but not quite
Our favourite what if
Oh how I wished that you could lived
One day I hope we will be there and you will be with us too
No matter if we ever have another we will always remember you

In memory of; Baby H 3rd November 2022

LOCKDOWN

Lock down said Boris
You must stay at home
Unless of course you can't
And then you must roam

You can't go to work
Unless we need you too
Work from home if you can
But if you can't then do

Que for the shops but only if you must
Ideally get deliveries just don't make a fuss
Two metres apart is the safest distance
But it doesnt apply for teachers, Dr's or dentists

You can't have your hair cut or go for a swim
The park is closed where to begin?
You can not drive or go outside
Unless you need to test your eyes
You can't gather in groups of more than six
Unless you have wine & cheese and its a fix

If you live alone you can go see your mum
But if you live with someone sorry your done
Households can't mix except when rules say they can

And sing happy birthday when washing your hands

Bake your banana bread
Teach the children on zoom
Do everything Boris said
But your all in one room

Lock down Is lifted but we're now in a zone
Maybe we should wear masks, who'd have known
You must wear a mask when your standing inside or out
But if your sitting down take it off what's that all about?

You can go to the pub but must be home by ten
The virus will get you if your out after then.
If you have it you must isolate for ten days or more
And those who you live with must also stay in doors!

Then the vaccine strong and true
Here to end Lock down for me and you
Conspiracy theories of tracking and 5G
Lockdown has driven us mad you see

Stand in line for a jab in your arm
Don't worry we don't think it will cause any harm
You have to have it or this will never end
But it's entirely your choice that you don't have to defend.

Lockdown is over you can now leave your home
Eat out to help out so businesses grow
Staycations are on and the parks are packed
It's time for some politicians to be sacked.

A summer of fun good weather and all
But now comes the graphs as we enter the fall
The weather turns colder and cases they rise
The vaccines are back and we all just surmise
That the vaccine will mean we carry on as we are
But another lockdown is never far.

Christmas arrives but for most it is dull
As a lockdown in zone 3's has just begun

By the turn of the year were all locked down again
And Boris is telling us we can beat it but when?
By the end of May of 2021 the lockdowns are all done
The rebuilding of society has finally begun.

The way we were...

I visit you regularly
Your physically there
Although i know
In your mind you're elsewhere

The person you were is locked inside
You forget who I am so I try to remind
I tell of the times we shared together
Memories I thought would last forever

I wash and dress you the tides have turned
I feed and help you the favours returned
Of the thankless tasks of raising your child
With love and care you were always kind.

I think of the times when I was young
And my life had only just begun
The times you pushed me on the swing
And the squeals of laughter that would bring

When i grew up and started school
You took me there and collected me too
For every event your face in the crowd
Would quieten the fear no matter how loud

I left my primary school moved onto adventures new
The support from you only grew
Through teenage strops and heartbreak too
The one to fix it all was always you.

On the day I married you were there again
Not losing a daughter but a son to gain
Soon we had a child of our own
Oh how you adored watching them grow.

As they grew up and flew the nest
I knew that you were not at your best
Where's my keys? the sugar? the loo?
I tried to help but I didn't know what to do

The person I'd relied on all my life was fading fast
Living not in the now but more in the past
And while it's frustrating for me to see
I know that your content to just be

So I stop correcting you when you're wrong
I listen to the stories one by one
I've heard them all a thousand times before
And I'll hear them a hundred more.

Dementia has taken the mum I once had
But my memories are safe and of that I'm glad

There's days I wish you could understand
So I could tell you your the best mum I could ever of had
This disease and its progress is frustrating it's true
But mum I hope you know how much I love you!

Marriage

Once upon a time (not long ago) in a land far away, (Jarrow)
A couple joined hands, on their wedding day.
They vowed to love each other, in sickness and in health,
Little did they know, it would be a comedy of stealth.

The honeymoon phase, oh, it was a blast,
They thought their love would forever last.
But soon enough, reality hit with a smack,
As they discovered quirks, they couldn't retract.

Socks on the floor not in the laundry bin
What to watch on TV where to begin
The toilet seat, a never-ending debate,
Up or down, it was their daily fate.

They bickered over blankets, snoring, and space,
Each night, a battlefield, in their cozy place.
He'll drive her crazy won't pick up his smalls
He'll lie in, get drunk and scratch at his balls
She'll nag him, go shopping for nothing they need
Leave hair in the shower
how can this succeed?

Yet, in the midst of chaos, they found a way,
To laugh through the madness, day after day.

They learned to compromise, to give and to take,
To find joy in the silly moments they'd make.
They embraced each quirk and idiosyncrasy,
For laughter was their secret recipe.

They turned mishaps into anecdotes to share,
Creating memories, beyond compare.

For marriage, you see, is a humorous dance,
A mix of laughter, love and hardwork not chance
It's finding joy in the absurd and mundane
Forgiving quickly and trying again.

So here's to marriage, with all its wacky charms,
A journey filled with laughter, in each other's
arms.
Through laughter and love, they'll conquer each
day,
For in humor's embrace, their marriage will
forever stay.

For my happily ever after
Jamie Hiscock

Born Still

There's a hole created that nothing can fill
The moment your child is born still!
The hopes, imaginings and dreams are gone
Those milestones you hoped for suddenly there's none
There's a life to be grieved for though a breath was never taken
There's an intense sort of love that can't be forsaken.
People look away they don't want to know
The pain of losing something before it had chance to grow.
There's no name for a parent who loses a child,
It's not supposed to happen so words are hard to find.
My world has altered how can it be
That everything is normal around me

My life as I knew it has ended its true
It's now in two half's before and after you
I want to move forward but I'm scared to forget
I want to remember the good not be filled with regret
Grief is now my partner with me wherever I go

It's only here because i loved you, this much I know.
I still wish I had you here on earth with me
But you show me that your with me in lots of ways I see.
The white butterfly that we see everywhere
A White feather that appears when no others are there
There's always going to be a space that nothing else can fill
That's because that space is yours even though you were born still!

For Elijah Freddie Hiscock
Our Angel

Midwife

In the depths of sorrow's embrace,
A bereavement midwife, a guiding grace.
With gentle hands and a compassionate heart,
She tends to souls torn apart.

When grief arrives it takes over love there's
nothing left to say
She walks alongside those who've lost, and helps
them find their way.

With tender words and empathetic eyes,
She listens to stories, she hears their cries.
She holds their hands, shares in their pain,
Guiding them through sorrow's terrain.

A footprint on the paper and hair into the box
Precious lasting memories not enough but all
they've got
She honors their memories, their precious ones,
Helping them find solace when hope seems
gone.

Another funeral, a precious child lost
She holds it together at all costs
Knowing so personally the weight of the pain
She hugs the mother who breaks down again.

She walks beside them on the path of grief,
A guardian angel, offering relief.
She provides support, both day and night.
A pillar of strength, shining bright.

For in the midst of loss and pain,
She brings comfort, she shares the strain
A guardian of souls, in their darkest hour,
A bereavement midwife, embodying power.
They never want to meet her yet are greatful when they do
She meets them on the worst day and carries them through.
From the depths of despair to the glimmers of hope she stands as their guide
Blood tests, injections, post mortem, live births she will stay at their bedside.
Bereavement midwifes are angels it's true
We got the best when we got you!

For Jamie Renilson
Bereavement midwife

The Room

I sit in a room feeling so alone
I wish I had the chance to see you grown
Instead your life was barely started
Then you were gone and we were left broken
hearted.
People tell us how sorry they are
They are thinking of us from near and far

The Dr's they say it was just one of those things
Without realising the anguish those words bring
It's just bad luck you can just try again
It's sad right now but you'll get through the pain.
It's just not meant to be something was wrong
Better it was now and not further along

This is not normal and it shouldn't be the case
That tragedies like this are treat like common
place.

I leave the hospital in my hands is a Box
with mementos of the baby to mark the loss
There are no visitors they leave us to grieve
I feel so robbed I feel so deceived.

There are no cards no congratulations for me
Because clearly I'd failed and it wasn't to be.
I won't get over this I'll learn to live with it sure
But I'm not the same person I was before.

I sit at home in an empty room that should be
filled with you
Though I know that your not coming home
there's nothing else I can do!

Show me you are with us that you are flying free
Until the day that I come home and you can run
to me
I'll hold you and I'll kiss you I'll never let you
go
I'll tell you that we always loved you though I'm
sure you already know!

Funeral director

In somber halls where grief resides,
Among the sorrow that sadness hides,
There stand the ones who bring solace near,
Funeral directors compassionate, sincere.

With tender hearts and gentle grace,
They navigate this solemn space,
They listen to stories, memories they share
Offering empathy showing they care

The phone is ringing
The door is dinging
There's devastation everywhere
with the grace of a Swan they take it in they
juggle it all they're there!
They care for those no longer here
They care for the ones they held most dear
With a smile, an ear and cuppa on the go
Having a chat, answering questions we always
know
They fix it all with gentle care
Day or night they're always there

One chance to get this right the weight of
responsibility they bare

Making sure details are finite to really show they care
Arranging the service, with utmost respect,
Creating a tribute, memories reflect.

From tiny babies who were born asleep
To war veterans their rooms they keep
A place for family with poems and flowers too
For the time that they are with them then it starts anew

Their hands, steady, as they guide the way,
Supporting those who mourn, day by day,
In their presence, we find relief,
A soothing balm, amidst our grief,
In a time of chaos they are the calm place
In the eye of the storm they are a safe space

So let us honor these unsung heroes,
Whose compassion and kindness flows,
For in their service, they give their all,
Answering life's final call.
For
Gill & Jarrow Funeral care

The mask

When you look at me what do you see?
When you stop and stare what are you hoping to find there?
Yes I am swaying or flapping my hands
Maybe I'm spinning or throwing the sand
I'm trying to regulate what's inside
And your stares make me want to hide
Hide who I am so no one knows
The turmoil inside as I start to grow
The mask just grows thicker with each passing day
So I don't have those looks thrown my way
I'm exhausted by living not lazy or boring
Just totally burnt put from the pretending the ignoring
So I stay inside and sleep when I can
I have the heating blasting and sit next to the fan
I eat one type of food that I know is good but
then people come in and tell me I should
Eat better food it would help me feel good and
go outside to get vitamin D in my blood.
I tell them of the looks and stares out there
But they tell me to ignore them that I shouldn't care

but really let's face it they shouldn't be there.
In a society that claims its inclusive
why is it that this is so elusive
people are who they are they aren't broken or mad
and you staring and whispering only makes them feel bad.
You will forget your Stare in a day
but it stays with your subject in every way
When we try to remove the mask we forgot who we are
we try different things but we don't get far
'You don't look Autistic' someone will say
'You didn't act like that yesterday'
'Why you saying no when you usually say yes?'
'I'm finding my voice' you try and stress
'This is me I was hiding before now I'm being true to myself more'
'I liked you better before you were Autistic'
'Your milking it now' it drives you ballistic
'You did before you can do it again'
so you retreat back inside to save you the pain
put on the mask so all they see is success even if behind it your life is a mess!

My Best Friend

In the realm of friendship, a bond so true,
Lies the tale of best friends, me and you.
I wish that I could say that I met you back at school
A few extra years would have been cool.

As it is we met 8 years ago
At the PTA
When there was so much i didn't know and i didnt have a lot to say

It's fair to say my shyness made me come off as a stuck up cow
But I'm pleased you saw through it just look at us now.
Walks on the beach (handbag and all)
We talked and laughed at the rise and fall
Of parenthood, relationships and general life
You cheered me through the good
And drug me through the strife

When my fairytale came true and I was to be a bride
There was never any doubt who I wanted by my side.

We stayed up until the early hours
Talking dresses, food and flowers.
The day came round so quickly, the sun shone bright
We were so excited, we'd been up half the night.
You zipped up my dress and tied my shoes and
looked on with a smile as I said I do

From the highest of highs my life fell apart
You were there to catch me and help heal my heart.
Like a compass guiding through life's unknown,
We navigate together, never alone.

Through ups and downs, we stand side by side,
A bond resilient, with love as our guide.

So here's to you, my cherished friend,
A connection that time will never bend.
Through the years, our friendship will transcend,
Forever and always, my best friend.

For my long suffering best friend
Stacey Haslam

Happy

In a world of wonder, where joy resides,
A happy poem, let me provide.
With colors vibrant, and spirits bright,
I'll paint a picture of pure delight.

Sunbeams dance upon fields of green,
Where laughter echoes, a blissful scene.
Butterflies flutter, spreading glee,
As nature's melody sets our hearts free.

Children's laughter fills the air,
Their innocence and wonder, beyond compare.
Their smiles infectious, like rays of sun,
Igniting happiness, for everyone.

Birds serenade with melodic tunes,
A chorus of joy beneath the moon.
Flowers bloom, a kaleidoscope of hues,
Their fragrance lifting spirits, as nature renews.

Friendship blooms, like petals unfurled,
With warmth and love, it lights the world.
Kindness shared, in each word and deed,
Creating a ripple of joy, a beautiful seed.

Celebrations ignite with cheer,
As loved ones gather, drawing near.
Toasting to life, in moments sublime,
Creating memories, frozen in time.

So let us revel in life's embrace,
With grateful hearts and a smiling face.
For happiness dwells within our reach,
In every moment, let us truly teach.

This happy poem, a gentle reminder,
That joy awaits us, in every kind encounter.
So let us cherish life's precious gift,
And spread happiness, as our spirits lift.

It doesn't end

Autistic children grow up you see
I bet your wondering what they will be
Well that depends on the here and now
On the support and understanding of how
How to help them in education
How to save them from manipulation
How to convince them that they are enough
How to give them a childhood so adult recovery isn't rough
Autistic adults look like you and me
They mask and hide behind the scene
It can all look ok from the outside in but from the inside out they don't know where to begin
Letters arrive but remain unopened
The washing pile grows but the machine sits unloaded

The millions of jobs that need to be done
But they're caught up in something that's fun
They try to socialise make friends say 'hi'
People they use them then tell them goodbye
They use all their energy to get themselves out
To be told they're weird or quirky what's that all about?
People are confusing this is true

They think but don't say and say but don't do
Autism isn't the tradgedy at play
It's ignorance that really ruins the day.

Wearing their masks making sure they don't slip
It becomes exhausting and their mental health
takes a dip

They want what everyone else has in life
A job, friends, a husband or wife
They just need small extra steps to be heard and
seen
autism doesn't dissappear at eighteen.
They are lots of Autistic adults
you wouldn't know to just look
In fact there is one right here
writing this book.

I see you

I see you there trying to hold it together
Pretending your world hasn't altered
I see you there saying your fine
No matter the question your response hasn't faltered

The trouble with that though is you almost believe
That nothing is wrong you have just been deceived
That the person you held so dearly in life has just quite simply gone
You can not accept that how will you go on!

I see you there making cups of tea
Handing out tissues and sympathy

I see you finally privately weep
And making promises you can't keep
You would do anything to have them back with you
It's just not possible no matter what you do.

I see you isolate yourself from the world
I wish you could listen so you could have heard

I've been in your shoes and I wear them each
day
They hurt me and pinch me in every way
Others they wear similar shoes to me
But there's seem more comfortable how can that
be?
Each step I take hurts me more
Every day worse than the one before
But I promise those shoes give a little each day
And they start to become tolerable In a strange
sort of way.
Somethings will detract from pain of the shoes
once they are worn and a little less new.

I see you there going through it all
I know you dont see me but please hear my call

I've worn my shoes for longer than you
And yes they still hurt me that much is true
But i do believe I will find some relief
If I just give it time it's the only thing for grief
I see you there doing all you can do
Please take care of yourself you matter too

I'm here

In the sky there's a darkness which matches your hearts
Im in a parallel universe where endings are starts
My light shone bright then dimmed it's glow
Dont worry about what you didnt say, i already know.

Cling to our memories don't let them pass
In time it will be like holding a looking glass
This is not goodbye that would bring too much pain
It's simply bye for now I will see you again
Through the hurt and silence and the tears of despair
If only you would look for me you'd see I'm always there.

I'm hiding in shadows where memories play
Lifting you up to face another day
Dancing in the moonlight with such delight
On the wings of a butterfly I take my flight

Now I dance among the starlight where no pain can reach or bind

Knowing always and forever our hearts are entwined.

As I sleep peacefully my lifes work done
My journey to eternity has now begun

Though your hearts are now aching we know we were blessed
The time we spent together it was just the best.

Baby loss awareness week

For one week we can speak of them
For one month we openly remember
Before long it's done again
Racing towards the excitement of December
To those who have not lost, its a like, a heart, a moment
For those of us who have it's a heart that's always broken.
The candles that we light for them burn for just one hour
Lighting them in unity seems to give us power
Our babies were here, however briefly, they were important too
Worth more than uncomfortable looks and a couple of days turning pink and blue

Say their names to parents it won't remind us I swear
We don't ever forget them the pain it is always there
Wether its been a week, a month, a year or more that day will be just as raw
So baby loss awareness week is just that awareness to the cause awareness of the fact

1 in 4 is not just a statistic it's a family changed
forever
It's something that we need to change by
standing here together
Share a post, sign a petition use Facebook
templates too,
But most importantly whatever you do
say the name of loved ones to their family
because their baby mattered too!

What is a parent carer

It's staying at home with our feet up all day,
While others work our wages they pay
Its getting the offers, the discounts and deals
All to help with our child's extra needs
It's the DLA we get for no reason
It's jumping the ques while others stand freezing
If only this perception was true
Here's the truth I'll tell you
It's the bruises we hide from the meltdown last night
From holding them until they had no more fight
Its the regimented life that we now live
For a family meal out what we wouldn't give
It's the sleep we don't get and the nights out we miss
It's the explanation to others about all of this
It's the fights that we face in every single way to get their needs met at the end of the day
Its the story you tell for the hundredth time to various people, you want to cry
It's the tears we hide because we're scared we're not coping
It's the smiles we paint on there's no use in moping

It's the splints we fit and the exercises we do
physio, nurse and chef we are too.
It's the appointments to remember with doctors
and dentist to be honest I'm not sure how were
not all demented.
It's the progress reviews we sit through at school
hearing all their struggles it all seems so cruel
Its the stares in the playground and the parties
they dont get asked too
It's explaining to them why after the 10th time
they've asked you
It's buying the 12th pair of shoes in a term
because our children destroy them when will
they learn
It's wanting to work but not having the time it's
the desperation to have something that's solely
mine
It's the not giving up when the going gets tough
Its a appreciating the smooth and riding the
rough
It's the smiles that they give you and the light in
their eyes
It's the ' I love you's' that take us by surprise
It's the others you meet in this new way of life
that gets you through the troubles and strife
It's the strength you didn't know you possessed
it's the times you went on even when you were
stressed

Its the love that you have for your child who is
special that gets us through these tasks
but some understanding and empathy from
others is not too much to ask!

Dedicated to all the parent carers out there.
You are amazing!

An autism Christmas

I came home, I was ready for my tea.
When I saw my mum decorating a tree
This would be crazy no matter what.
But I think that she's lost the plot.
This tree that she was wrapping with coloured lights that zoom
It was not outside but in our living room.

I went upstairs and, to my surprise,
My bedroom was wearing a disguise
My quilt had no dinos but santa instead
And a huge brown reindeer sat on my bed.
Oh no! This won't do something isn't right
But it didn't end there on that terrible night.
My dad brought a sock which he hung on my door.
It was really big, I didn't know who it was for.

It's for Santa to come with your presents, they said.
He will come and deliver them when you're in bed.
I don't want him to come, this jolly old guy.
Watching me sleep on reindeer that fly

I don't know who he is, but last week at some grotto
Mum told me to sit on his lap. That's against her motto.
Don't talk to strangers, she tells me regularly.
You must not go off with anyone without telling me.
But this man had a beard and wore a red coat.
Handed out presents wrapped up with a bow
I sat there and smiled while the camera flashed.
Then he handed me a box from the ones he had stashed

When I awoke Christmas morning, I wanted my drink.
But mum and dad told me to wait. I didn't know what to think.
They shouted me down to where the tree was living.
Under it there was wrapped up boxes to be given

The lights were flashing and the music was loud.
My parents just stood there looking proud.
I had enough. I could take no more.

The change, too much I fell to the floor.
My nanny arrived with another box in her hand.
I looked at her, pleading for her to understand.

She scooped me up and hugged me tight.
Whispered to me, it would be alright
I sat at the table and had my drink.
While nanny washed the dishes in the kitchen sink.
Then I went back to the living room.
With a sense of impending doom
The lights were off and it was noisy no more.
No boxes, but just gifts I'd asked for.
I hugged my mum and then my dad
I smiled at them all, especially my nan.

Christmas is different for everyone.
But I'm sure you all agree
After the food and the gifts are all gone
We only remember who is around the tree.

Milton Keynes UK
Ingram Content Group UK Ltd.
UKHW020627270524
443037UK00021B/656

9 789358 316568